ENGINEERING CHALLENGES
BUILDING STADIUMS

by Rebecca Rowell

FOCUS READERS

WWW.FOCUSREADERS.COM

Focus Readers is distributed by North Star Editions:
sales@northstareditions.com | 888-417-0195

Produced for Focus Readers by Red Line Editorial.

Content Consultant: Ryan Hopeman, PE, SE, Practice Director at Meyer Borgman Johnson, and adjunct professor at the University of Minnesota College of Design

Photographs ©: Scruggelgreen/Shutterstock Images, cover, 1; Scott Boehm/AP Images, 4–5; haoliang/iStockphoto, 7; felixmizioznikov/iStockphoto, 8; toddmedia/iStockphoto, 10–11; narvikk/iStockphoto, 13; Darren Calabrese/The Canadian Press/AP Images, 15; fototrav/iStockphoto, 16; lev radin/Shutterstock Images, 18–19; Jimmie48 Photography/Shutterstock Images, 21; Cassiohabib/Shutterstock Images, 22–23; Red Line Editorial, 24–25, 27, 28

ISBN
978-1-63517-257-7 (hardcover)
978-1-63517-322-2 (paperback)
978-1-63517-452-6 (ebook pdf)
978-1-63517-387-1 (hosted ebook)

Library of Congress Control Number: 2017935929

Printed in the United States of America
Mankato, MN
June, 2017

ABOUT THE AUTHOR

Rebecca Rowell has worked on numerous books for young readers as an author and as an editor. Her writing includes titles about ancient India, Rachel Carson, John F. Kennedy, and the Louisiana Purchase. One of her favorite parts of writing is doing research and learning about all kinds of subjects. Rebecca has a master's degree in publishing and writing from Emerson College. She lives in Minneapolis, Minnesota.

TABLE OF CONTENTS

CHAPTER 1

A SIGHT TO BEHOLD

Fans could not believe their eyes. After two years of construction, US Bank Stadium in Minneapolis, Minnesota, opened to the public. Now it was time to watch a Minnesota Vikings football game. At 270 feet (82 m) tall, the stadium towered over fans. A huge glass wall greeted visitors at the main entrance.

US Bank Stadium opened in the summer of 2016.

A roof kept fans protected from rain, snow, wind, and cold. But the roof still allowed light into the stadium. Fans felt like they were outdoors.

Today's stadiums are more than just places to watch sports and concerts. They are state-of-the-art structures. It hasn't always been this way, though.

Humans have built stadiums for centuries. For example, the ancient Romans built the Colosseum nearly 2,000 years ago. But its design is not outdated. Stadiums today have the same basic footprint.

The Colosseum is made of stone and **concrete**. Modern stadiums use concrete.

The Roman Colosseum hosted gladiatorial combats many years ago.

Many use steel, too. Steel is a strong but relatively lightweight metal. It allows engineers to span much longer distances, such as the US Bank Stadium roof.

Modern stadiums, such as Marlins Park in Florida, are more advanced than ever before.

Other changes have affected the stadium experience. Comfortable chairs have replaced simple benches or earth **berms**. Most stadiums today also have lights, scoreboards, and other electronic elements. Some newer stadiums even have hotels, restaurants, and offices inside them.

Stadiums must be designed to host events. Different sports have different needs for their stadiums. But modern engineers use their skills to create structures that do more than just house sporting events.

With new features and stunning design, many of today's stadiums are just as exciting as the events that take place inside them.

CHAPTER 2

THOUGHTFUL DESIGN, GREAT STADIUMS

The stadium design process begins with architects. They work with the owner of the stadium to plan the basic details. First they decide what the stadium will be used for. Then they determine its look and main features. Once the architects have a plan, the engineers help make it a reality by designing the structure.

The University of Alabama's Bryant-Denny Stadium seats more than 100,000 fans.

All stadiums must be safe. To help ensure this, engineers consider different loads. Dead load is the weight of the building itself. Floors, walls, and ceilings figure into a stadium's dead load. Live load is the weight of the items that could change over time. This includes things such as people inside the building. Environmental loads could include wind, rain, snow, and earthquakes.

Engineers make sure the stadium is built on a firm foundation that can handle these loads. If the loads are too high, the soil may settle. Engineers adjust for different types of soil to prevent the stadium from settling too much.

The San Francisco Giants' baseball park is built along San Francisco Bay.

Building codes are an important tool. These are minimum safety requirements set by the government. Engineers need to be familiar with these codes. They use the codes to help guide their designs.

Engineers select materials for a stadium. They look for materials that are strong. But they also consider cost, environment, and appearance. Wood, for example, is not as strong as concrete or steel. But it's lightweight and cheaper.

Climate affects a stadium's design. For example, many stadiums now have roofs. The roof might be flat, or it might be a dome. Some baseball and football stadiums have fully **retractable** roofs. They can be closed on cold or rainy days. Climate also influences a stadium's environmental load. In colder areas, an engineer might need to design a roof that can support snow or ice in the winter.

The Rogers Centre in Toronto, Ontario, opened in 1989. It was the first stadium to have a fully retractable roof.

Builders are also making stadiums more energy **efficient**. Lincoln Financial Field in Philadelphia, Pennsylvania, is one of the most energy efficient. It has **wind turbines** and thousands of **solar panels**. These help the stadium produce its own electricity.

The 2008 Olympic stadium in Beijing, China, was designed to inspire.

Money also affects some decisions. A stadium project will have a budget. Certain materials or features might need to be left out to stay on budget.

All these elements come together during the design process. The result is a stadium unlike any other. Next, workers must make the design a reality.

ENGINEERING DESIGN PROCESS

Stadiums are complex buildings. Engineers must be confident in their plans. They use various tools and codes in their planning. This helps them make sure the final stadium meets expectations.

ASK: What are the expectations for this stadium? What type of events will it host? How many people does it need to hold? What materials are needed?

IMAGINE: Look at other stadiums for ideas. What ideas could be borrowed? What are some new ideas that will make this stadium stand out?

PLAN: Draw a diagram. Models are also helpful.

CREATE: Follow the plan and build the stadium. How does it look?

IMPROVE: What works? What doesn't? What could work better? Modify the design to make it stronger.

CHAPTER 3

FACING TECHNICAL CHALLENGES

Sometimes a stadium needs change. That was the case with Arthur Ashe Stadium. The tennis facility opened in 1997 in Flushing, New York. It hosts the US Open each summer. However, rain often interfered with the tournament. So in 2016, a roof was added to the stadium.

Arthur Ashe Stadium was built without a roof.

Adding a roof posed many challenges. Arthur Ashe Stadium was built on marshy ground. It wouldn't support a heavy roof. So engineers and architects instead designed a separate structure that would go around the existing stadium.

The structure has eight steel **columns**. They are supported by **piles** driven 175 feet (53 m) underground. This holds up the roof. The roof includes two panels. The panels each weigh 500 short tons (454 metric tons). But they can open and close. The panels move on wheels set in rails. Cables pull the panels open. Fully opening the panels takes approximately seven minutes.

A match takes place under the roof at Arthur Ashe Stadium.

The roof is helpful during rainy weather. But enclosing the stadium presents a problem. Condensation forms quickly. To keep water from dripping on people in the stadium, workers installed a cooling system. Machines send cool air through a **duct**. The cool air helps prevent condensation.

GOLDEN 1 CENTER

The Sacramento Kings basketball team moved into Golden 1 Center in 2016. When creating the venue, electrical engineers had visitors in mind. The stadium has more than 1,000 Wi-Fi hotspots. The hotspots provide Wi-Fi and cellular coverage for more than 1 million square feet (92,900 sq. m). Workers installed more than 300 miles (483 km) of copper wire as well as 650 miles (1,046 km) of fiber-optic cable to power this system. The stadium even has a data center.

Golden 1 Center's technology also includes audio and visual elements. Twenty-four speakers provide surround sound. Sports fans can watch replays on a screen measuring 84 feet (26 m).

Engineers wanted to give Golden 1 Center the most advanced technology of any stadium.

CHAPTER 4

BUILD IT

Stadiums have many different kinds of roofs. Using strips of paper, build a colorful roof for your own shoebox stadium.

Materials:

You'll need a shoebox, construction paper, and some scissors. You can add additional decorations if you'd like.

You can create many different roof shapes simply by using strips of paper.

Procedure:

1. Remove the lid from your shoebox. Pretend the open shoebox is an open-air stadium. But the stadium's owner wants to add a roof.

2. Cut the construction paper into narrow strips. They should be about 1 inch (2.5 cm) wide.

3. Place the paper strips over the shoebox to create a colorful roof for your stadium. Consider different designs. Try to come up with a roof that is both sturdy and unique.

Considerations:

- There are many different types of roofs. Do you want yours to be fully

This stadium has a woven roof that stays together without using tape.

or partially enclosed? Should it be flat or rounded? How much natural light should it let in?

- A roof needs to be sturdy. Does yours stay together on its own?

By adding beams made of folded paper, the woven roof became both sturdier and more open.

Improve It!

You've made a colorful roof. Now make it even better. Try changing your design so that your roof is even sturdier.

- Are there stronger designs you can create with your paper strips?
- What happens if you include wider strips of paper in your design? Try folding them. How can folded paper improve your design?
- Have a friend blow against the roof as hard as he or she can. Did the roof stay standing? If not, improve it.
- Try setting your scissors on the roof. Is the roof strong enough to hold the scissors?

FOCUS ON
BUILDING STADIUMS

Write your answers on a separate piece of paper.

1. Write a letter to a friend describing what you learned about retractable stadium roofs.

2. Do you think engineers should do more to make stadiums energy efficient? Why or why not?

3. Which famous stadium did the ancient Romans build nearly 2,000 years ago?

    A. Arthur Ashe Stadium
    B. Olympic Stadium
    C. the Colosseum

4. What could happen if engineers build a stadium on a weak foundation?

    A. The stadium might catch on fire.
    B. The stadium might sink into the ground.
    C. The stadium might not look as exciting.

Answer key on page 32.

GLOSSARY

berms
Raised mounds of land.

columns
Vertical posts that support horizontal objects such as floors and roofs.

concrete
A strong, stonelike material made from gravel, sand, cement, and water.

duct
A metal tube used to carry air.

efficient
Accomplishing as much as possible with as little effort or resources as possible.

piles
Structural elements that are driven into the ground to reach stronger soil than is available at the surface.

retractable
Able to be moved.

solar panels
Tools that convert sunlight into electricity.

wind turbines
Structures that create electricity from the wind.

TO LEARN MORE

BOOKS

Graham, Ian. *Amazing Stadiums*. Mankato, MN: Amicus, 2011.

Hurley, Michael. *The World's Most Amazing Stadiums*. Chicago: Raintree, 2012.

Mann, Elizabeth. *The Roman Colosseum: The Story of the World's Most Famous Stadium and Its Deadly Games*. Richmond Hill, ON: Mikaya Press, 2006.

NOTE TO EDUCATORS

Visit **www.focusreaders.com** to find lesson plans, activities, links, and other resources related to this title.

INDEX